DOWN TO EARTH OBSERVATIONS

ON THE BEAUTY OF LIFE

COMPILED FROM AND INSPIRED BY

THE PRONOUNCEMENTS OF

J. KRISHNAMURTI

*

THE UNIQUENESS OF THIS <u>LIVING</u> BOOKLET
LIES IN THE FACT THAT THESE REFERENCES
ARE NOT MERE SENTENCES TAKEN FROM PUBLISHED TEXTS
*

BUT INSTEAD THEY PRESENT IN A VERSE-LIKE FORM
A SELECTION OF KRISHNAMURTI'S STATEMENTS
THEREBY BRINGING OUT THE CORE OF HIS MESSAGE

*

THE EXTENSIVE BIBLIOGRAPHY ALLOWS THE READER
FURTHERMORE TO EASILY REFER TO
KRISHNAMURTI'S ORIGINAL STATEMENTS
FOR FURTHER ORIENTATION

I

SECOND EDITION

SECOND PRINTING 1988

PUBLISHED BY

(THE *WHAT-IS* PRESS)®

WOODSTOCK N.Y. 12498

U.S.A.

COPYRIGHT © 1986–1988

by J. C. van Rijn

ISBN 0-9617483-3-8

Manufactured in the USA
Printed by Rose Printing Co., Inc.

ACKNOWLEDGEMENT

THE COMPILER HEREBY GRATEFULLY
ACKNOWLEDGES THE SEVERAL PUBLISHERS
FROM WHOSE PUBLICATIONS WERE CULLED
MOST OF KRISHNAMURTI'S STATEMENTS
HERE ASSEMBLED

THE FRONT COVER

THE FRONT COVER REPRESENTS PICTORIALLY
THE LAST WORDS KRISHNAMURTI SPOKE TO ME
IN A PRIVATE INTERVIEW AND WHICH ARE
THE SUBJECT OF PAGE 1 IN THIS BOOKLET

FRONT COVER DESIGN BY
PAT KELLY, WOODSTOCK, NY

INTRODUCTION

The longer I have read Krishnamurti's published talks over a period of 52 years, the more I have become impressed by the validity of his statements. The justification for this booklet lays in the fact that such repeated contact with the salient points of Krishnamurti's statements brought forth a growing impact and understanding, well beyond what the particular text had meant to me at the time of first hearing or reading.

The contents of this booklet should not be read in the normal sense of the word, instead experienced; and at times when the mind is passive and quiet, fully alert and receptive. The best times could well be when retiring, or even better when awakening in the morning; better still, when one happens to wake up in the middle of the night. (p. 38 & 39)

To avoid distraction, each page contains one argument only and the booklet can be laid open flat, the opposite page remaining blank and could be used for notes. At first reading many of these statements may leave you with some disbelief and questions, while repeated reading will bring forth an ever fuller awareness and insight.

This booklet is not meant to replace the published full texts of Krishnamurti's talks and writings, therefore each of the condensed statements is fitted with a footnote referring to a section in the rear of the booklet giving: title, publisher, date of publication and number of page involved. This allows the reader to refer, at any time, to the full original text, which could lead to more readily grasping the full impact of Krishnamurti's sayings. Such original publications are available at libraries and bookstores and from the 3 Krishnamurti Foundations:

U.S.A.: OJAI P. O. Box 1560, CA 93023
INDIA: 64/5 Greenways Road, Madras 600028
ENGLAND: Brockwood Park — Bramdean Hants SO24.OLQ

One can hardly expect to absorb the contents of this booklet in one reading, but the satisfaction will be to be able to return to it repeatedly for new insights. It may become a constant companion, as it has been to me.

J. C. van Rijn

INDEX BY SUBJECT

INDEX BY SUBJECT

TO SET MAN FREE

ON AUGUST 3rd 1929
AT THE OPENING OF THE STAR CAMP
AT OMMEN IN HOLLAND
KRISHNAMURTI DECLARED:

*

I AM CONCERNING MYSELF
WITH ONLY ONE ESSENTIAL THING
THAT IS
TO SET MAN FREE
ABSOLUTELY AND UNCONDITIONALLY[1]

*   *   *

PERSONALITY CULT

SHOULD YOU PERSONALLY
WORSHIP THE SPEAKER
THEN EVERYTHING HE IS SAYING
IS THEREBY CONTRADICTED

*

INSTEAD PARTICIPATE
IN WHAT THE SPEAKER IS SAYING[1]

*   *   *

LOOK FOR YOURSELF

ONLY WHEN YOU DENY THE AUTHORITY OF

THE TEACHERS

THE GURUS

THE MAHATMAS

THE PHILOSOPHERS

THE THEORETICIANS

HOWEVER WISE THEY MAY BE

INCLUDING J. KRISHNAMURTI

*

THEN YOU CAN LOOK FOR YOURSELF

BE BOTH YOUR PUPIL AND TEACHER

AND FIND OUT WHAT-IS[1]

* * *

THEREFORE

DOUBT

EVERYTHING

KRISHNAMURTI

SAYS[2]

* * *

CATEGORY NO. 1

THE OPPORTUNITIES WHILE LIVING

BEWARE OF IDEOLOGIES

BEING SOMEBODY

RELATIONSHIPS

THE BEAUTY OF LIFE

*

= Pages 1 to 12 =

*   *   *

NOTE

The following 108 pages have been broken down into eight
consecutively numbered categories. These categories are not strict and
are often overlapping, but may be helpful.

THE PLOWED FIELD

LIFE RESEMBLES A PLOWED FIELD

AWAITING TO BE SOWED

BY THE POSSIBILITIES OFFERED IN LIFE

* *

MAY THE STATEMENTS

HERE ASSEMBLED

STIMULATE THE SOWING[1]

* * *

DOING OUR PART

TO DO OUR PART

IN THE EVOLUTION OF THE HUMAN RACE

WE HAVE TO START WITH OURSELVES

OBSERVE OUR BEHAVIOR IN OUR RELATIONSHIPS

AVOID ISOLATION, DIVISION AND CONFLICT

REALIZE THAT WE INDIVIDUALLY

ARE THE WORLD[1]

* * *

DON'T ASK

WHAT IS THE PURPOSE OF LIFE

IT IS LIKE A BLIND MAN ASKING

WHAT IS LIGHT?

HE WILL LISTEN TO MY ANSWER

ACCORDING TO HIS BLINDNESS OR DARKNESS

* *

BUT FROM THE MOMENT HE IS ABLE TO SEE

HE WILL NEVER ASK WHAT IS LIGHT:

IT IS THERE![1]

* * *

SIGNIFICANCE OF LIFE

RELIGIOUS PEOPLE HAVE SAID THAT LIFE
IS ONLY A MEANS TO AN END
NON-RELIGIOUS PEOPLE MAINTAIN THAT
LIFE IS MEANINGLESS
STILL OTHERS HAVE INVENTED A SIGNIFICANCE
ACCORDING TO THEIR INTELLECT
OR CONDITIONING

*

INSTEAD ONE SHOULD OBSERVE LIFE
UN-EMOTIONALLY
AND UN-SENTIMENTALLY
WITHOUT ASSIGNING IT
ANY PARTICULAR SIGNIFICANCE

*   *

THEREBY DISCOVERING
THE BEAUTY AND VASTNESS
OF ITS POSSIBILITIES

*   *

THEN, ALSO, SHALL WE SUDDENLY UNDERSTAND
THE REAL AND FULL MEANING OF LOVE
AND SIMULTANEOUSLY THAT OF DEATH[1]

*   *   *

IDEOLOGY

THOUGHT FORMULATES A CONCEPT
ACCORDING TO WHICH WE TRY TO LIVE
AN IDEOLOGY

*

IDEOLOGIES HAVE CREATED
THE WORLD'S GREAT CONTROVERSIES
RELIGIONS, NATIONALITIES, AND MOVEMENTS
RESULTING IN HATE, VIOLENCE AND WARS[1]

*   *   *

IDEALS

THE PURSUIT OF AN IDEAL
PREVENTS HUMILITY
FOR SUCH PURSUIT
IS THE GLORIFICATION OF THE SELF[2]

*   *   *

BEING SOMEBODY

SO YOU PURSUE THE OUTER SHOW
WITHOUT THE INNER SUBSTANCE
SO DOES ANOTHER

*

YOU WITH YOUR IDEOLOGY OF BEING SOMEBODY
ARE AS INSUFFICIENT AS THE OTHER FELLOW
AND YOU WILL BE DESTROYING EACH OTHER
IN THE NAME OF
PEACE, SUFFICIENCY, ADEQUATE EMPLOYMENT
OR THE NAME OF GOD[1]

*   *   *

<u>THE POWER OF AN IDEA</u>

THE POWER OF AN IDEA

AND THE POWER OF THE SWORD

ARE SIMILAR

*   *

IDEA AND BELIEF

ARE THE ANTITHESIS OF LOVE[1]

*   *   *

RELATIONSHIP IS LIVING

LIFE IS A MOVEMENT IN RELATIONSHIP

THROUGH RELATIONSHIP WE LIVE

*

ISOLATION IS LIVING DEATH

IN RELATIONSHIP ALONE

CAN ONE OBSERVE ONESELF

*   *

LOVE IS THE GUIDING FORCE IN LIVING[1]

*   *   *

<u>BEING TOTALLY INVOLVED BUT UNCOMMITTED</u>

FACING THE DISORDER, HATRED AND BRUTALITY

IN THE WORLD AT LARGE

THERE IS THE URGE TO BE COMMITTED

TO POLITICAL, SOCIOLOGICAL OR RELIGIOUS

MOVEMENTS

THEREBY BECOMING PREDOMINENTLY INVOLVED

IN SOME PART OF THE WORLD'S TROUBLES

*   *

INSTEAD ONE SHOULD BE INVOLVED

TOTALLY

WITH THE ENTIRE PROBLEM OF LIVING

THEN ACTION IS ENTIRELY DIFFERENT

BOTH INWARD AND OUTWARDLY

*   *

BEING TOTALLY INVOLVED

IN ONE'S RELATIONSHIP WITH ONE'S SURROUNDING

WITHOUT BEING COMMITTED

TO ANY IDEA OR IDEOLOGY

WILL AVOID

DIVISION AND CONFLICT[1]

*   *   *

THE BEAUTY OF LIVING

WHEN NOT GIVING

A MEANING OR SIGNIFICANCE TO LIFE

WE WILL SEE THE BEAUTY OF LIVING

THE VERY VASTNESS OF IT

*   *

WITHOUT UNDERSTANDING WHAT LIVING IS

WE SHALL NOT BE ABLE TO UNDERSTAND

WHAT DYING IS

NOR WHAT LOVE IS[1]

*   *   *

BEWARE OF HOPE

A MIND THAT IS BURDENED WITH HOPE

IS ALREADY BIASED

AND CANNOT SEE

WITH CLARITY OF PERCEPTION

ACTUALLY "WHAT-IS"[1]

* * *

HUMANITY

WHEN YOU FULLY REALIZE THAT YOU ARE

THE REST OF MANKIND

IT BRINGS A TREMENDOUS ENERGY

*

YOU HAVE BROKEN THROUGH THE NARROW GROOVE

OF INDIVIDUALITY

AND THE NARROW CIRCLE OF

THE "ME" AND "YOU"

THE "WE" AND "THEY"[1]

*   *   *

CATEGORY NO. 2

LOVE

UNITY OF MANKIND

WHAT LOVE IS NOT

BEING VIRTUOUS

FUNDAMENTAL REVOLUTION

*

= Pages 13 to 29 =

*   *   *

PLENITUDE OF LOVE

ONLY A MIND AND A HEART

THAT ARE FULL OF LOVE

CAN SEE THE WHOLE MOVEMENT OF LIFE

*

THEN WHATEVER HE DOES

A MAN WHO POSSESSES SUCH LOVE

IS

MORAL, GOOD

AND WHAT HE DOES

IS BEAUTIFUL[1]

*   *   *

<u>LOVE</u>

LOVE IS
THAT EXTRAORDINARY THING
THAT TAKES PLACE
WHEN THERE IS NO "ME"
WITHIN ITS CIRCLE OR WALL[1]

*　　*　　*

LOVE'S DIMENSION

A DIMENSION THAT IS NOT

A PROJECTION OF ONE'S OWN LITTLE MIND

IT IS NOT PUT TOGETHER

BY THOUGHT[1]

* *

LOVE IS

THE VERY ESSENCE

OF THE ABSOLUTE[2]

* * *

EXPERIENCING LOVE

TO LOVE IS TO EXPERIENCE ALL THINGS

*

BUT TO EXPERIENCE WITHOUT LOVE
IS TO LIVE IN VAIN

*

LOVE IS VULNERABLE
BUT TO EXPERIENCE WITHOUT VULNERABILITY
IS TO STRENGTHEN DESIRE
DESIRE IS NOT LOVE — DESIRE CANNOT HOLD LOVE
ONLY LOVE CAN TAME DESIRE

*

LOVE IS NOT OF THE MIND
THE MIND MUST CEASE FOR LOVE TO BE[1]

*   *   *

UNITY OF MANKIND

THE ONLY WAY

TO REACH THE ESSENTIAL UNITY OF MANKIND

IS THE WAY OF LOVE

LOVE IS BEYOND THE TURMOIL OF THOUGHT

LOVE IS OF A DIFFERENT DIMENSION[1]

* *

MATURITY

THE HIGHEST FORM OF MATURITY

IS THE ENDING OF SELF INTEREST[2]

* * *

<u>CULTIVATING LOVE</u>

YOU CANNOT COME UPON LOVE

BY A PROCESS OF IDENTIFICATION

OR BY

ANY CULTIVATION OF THE MIND

OR BY

ANY CONSCIOUS EFFORT

* *

A MIND KNOWING ONLY THE PROCESS OF TIME

CANNOT RECOGNIZE LOVE

LOVE BEING NOT OF TIME[1]

* * *

<u>LOVE'S MOTIVE</u>

THE ACTION OF LOVE

HAS NO MOTIVE

EVERY OTHER ACTION HAS[1]

*   *

IDEA AND BELIEF ARE

THE VERY ANTITHESIS OF LOVE[2]

*   *   *

<u>FUNDAMENTAL REVOLUTION</u>

LOVE IS THE ONLY FACTOR

THAT CAN BRING ABOUT

A FUNDAMENTAL REVOLUTION

*   *

LOVE IS THE ONLY TRUE REVOLUTION[3]

*   *   *

LOVE AND AMBITION

LOVE BEING

THE ULTIMATE GUIDING FORCE IN LIFE

CAN AN AMBITIOUS MAN LOVE?

CAN A COMPETITIVE MAN LOVE?[1]

*   *

A MAN NEEDS FOOD, CLOTHING AND SHELTER

BUT WHEN THESE BECOME TO HIM

OF HIS GREATEST IMPORTANCE

THEN LOVE LOSES ITS MARVELOUS MEANING[2]

*   *

HOWEVER THIS DOES NOT EXCLUDE

THAT ONE MAY NEVERTHELESS ACT

AS IF

ONE WERE AMBITIOUS[3]

*   *   *

DEPENDENT LOVE

§ PETER "LOVES" RICE PUDDING.
PETER'S "LOVE" IS ENGENDERED BY AND
DEPENDENT ON RICE PUDDING.

§ PETER "LOVES" A STROLL IN THE WOODS.
PETER'S "LOVE" IS ENGENDERED BY AND
DEPENDENT ON THE WOODS.

§ PETER HAS "FALLEN IN LOVE" WITH THAT GIRL HE MET,
WHO RESPONDS TO HIS HUMOR, SHARES HIS PREJUDICES AND
IS PHYSICALLY HIS EQUAL. PETER'S "LOVE" IS ENGENDERED BY
AND DEPENDENT ON THIS GIRL.

§ PETER "LOVES" HIS WIFE, WHO COOKS HIS MEALS,
MENDS HIS SOCKS AND GIVES HIM PLEASURE IN BED.
BUT WHEN HIS WIFE HAS AN AFFAIR WITH ANOTHER MAN,
HE IS FURIOUS, HAS DONE WITH HIS "LOVE"
AND TREATS HER BADLY.

§ PETER IS A FAITHFUL RELIGIOUS WORSHIPPER,
HAS PROFOUND "LOVE" FOR HIS GOD,
WHO IS ALWAYS AVAILABLE TO HEAR HIS PRAYERS
AND, WITHOUT DEMANDING ANYTHING IN RETURN,
WILL NEVER TURN HIS BACK ON PETER.[1]

* * *

<u>WHAT LOVE IS NOT</u>

LOVE IN ITS TRUE SENSE

IS NOT

SENTIMENTALITY

OR

EMOTIONALISM

OR

ROMANTICISM

*

IT CANNOT PRODUCE

JEALOUSY

OR

ENVIOUSNESS

OR

POSSESSIVENESS[1]

*   *   *

<u>TRUE LOVE</u>

SUCH LOVE MAKES NO DISTINCTION
BETWEEN LOVE OF GOD OR LOVE OF MAN
OR LOVE OF THE ONE OR OF THE MANY
IT GIVES ITSELF ABUNDANTLY
WITHOUT DISCRIMINATION
AS A FLOWER GIVES ITS PERFUME[1]

*   *

SUCH LOVE CAN EXIST ONLY
WHEN THERE IS TOTAL FREEDOM FROM THE MIND
WHEN ALL ATTACHMENTS HAVE BEEN ABANDONED
LEADING TO EXTRAORDINARY STRENGTH[2]

*   *

MOST PEOPLE ARE AFRAID TO STAND ALONE
THEREFORE THEY SAY THEY LOVE GOD
BUT THIS IS NOT THE GOD UNKNOWN
THIS IS A THING CREATED BY THE MIND[3]

*   *   *

LOVE AND SPACE

WHEN YOU LOVE SOMETHING GREATLY

IN A NON-DEPENDENT SENSE

SPACE DISAPPEARS

THERE IS NO LONGER

AN "I" AND "IT"

OR AN "I" AND "YOU"

YOU "BECOME" THAT SOMETHING[1]

* * *

THE DIMENSION OF VIRTUE

VIRTUE MEANS TO LOVE

TO HAVE NO FEAR

TO LIVE AT THE HIGHEST LEVEL OF EXISTENCE

WHICH IS

TO DIE INWARDLY TO THE PAST

MAKING THE MIND CLEAR AND INNOCENT

* *

ONLY SUCH A MIND CAN COME UPON THIS

EXTRAORDINARY IMMENSITY

WHICH IS NOT OF YOUR OWN INVENTION

NOR THAT OF A PHILOSOPHER OR GURU[1]

* * *

BEING VIRTUOUS

CONDUCT BECOMES VIRTUOUS ONLY
WHEN THOUGHT DOES NOT CULTIVATE THAT
WHICH IT CONSIDERS TO BE VIRTUE
AND WHICH THEN BECOMES UNHOLY AND UGLY[1]

* *

SHOULD YOU PRACTICE VIRTUE
IT IS NO LONGER VIRTUE

*

YOU CANNOT CULTIVATE VIRTUE
ANYMORE THAN YOU CAN CULTIVATE
LOVE OR HUMILITY
VIRTUE WILL ONLY COME INTO BEING
AS A PRODUCT OF LOVE[2]

* * *

VIRTUE

IS NOT THE REPETITIVE BEHAVIOR

WHICH HAS BECOME RESPECTABLE

WITH THE ESTABLISHMENT[1]

★   ★   ★

VIRTUE IS SOMETHING

THAT CANNOT BE PURSUED

IT IS THEN AN ESCAPE FROM THE SELF

SUCH A PERSON HAS A NARROW MIND

WHICH IS NOT A VIRTUOUS MIND

★

THE MORE YOU TRY TO BECOME VIRTUOUS

THE MORE STRENGTH YOU GIVE TO THE "ME"[2]

★   ★   ★

VIRTUE

VIRTUE IS SOMETHING

THAT HAPPENS

FROM TIME TO TIME

LIKE BEAUTY

LIKE LOVE

*

IT IS NOT SOMETHING

YOU HAVE ACCUMULATED

AND FROM WHICH YOU ACT[1]

* * *

WHEN YOU SPEAK

LET YOUR WORDS PASS THE TEST

OF BEING ALL OF:

TRUTHFUL

+

KIND

+

HELPFUL

* * *

(Note: From Krishnamurti's very first published writing)[1]

CATEGORY NO. 3

BRAIN — MIND — THOUGHT

THINKING — CONSCIOUSNESS

ERUDITION — KNOWLEDGE — INTELLIGENCE

SCIENCE — INVENTION — CREATIVITY

*

* * *

XIII

THE NATURE OF THOUGHT

ACCUMULATED KNOWLEDGE AND EXPERIENCE
ARE THE INGREDIENTS OF THOUGHT

*

THOUGHT IS A MATERIAL PROCESS
THOUGHT IS NOTHING SPIRITUAL[1]

*   *   *

THE STILL MIND AND FREEDOM

CLARITY, INSIGHT AND UNDERSTANDING
ARE ONLY POSSIBLE
WHEN THOUGHT IS IN ABEYANCE

*

WHEN THE MIND IS STILL
FREEDOM PREVAILS[2]

*   *   *

INTELLECTUAL FREEDOM
IS THEREFORE ONLY ATTAINED
IN THE ABSENCE OF THOUGHT[3]

*   *   *

THOUGHT

THOUGHT IS THE MIND IN ACTION
MEMORIES ERUPT FROM THE BRAIN
IN THE FORM OF THOUGHT

*

A MIND THAT IS FREE
IS CAPABLE OF GOING IN ANY DIRECTION
UNBOUND BY THE PAST[1]

* * *

THE BRAIN

THE BRAIN IS A PHYSICAL MECHANISM
ESSENTIALLY THE SEAT OF THOUGHT

*

THE MIND IS DIFFERENT
IT HAS NO INVOLVEMENT IN THOUGHT AS TIME[2]

* * *

THE BRAIN AND THE MIND

THE BRAIN IS THE CENTER OF ALL OUR KNOWLEDGE

OUR THEORIES, OPINIONS AND PREJUDICES

AND OUR THOUGHTS AND FEARS

GATHERED BY US AND OUR FOREFATHERS

FOR 2 MILLION YEARS

*

THE BRAIN IS THE KEEPER

OF ALL OUR CONSCIOUSNESS

*   *

THE MIND CAN COMMUNICATE WITH THE BRAIN

BUT THE BRAIN CANNOT COMMUNICATE WITH THE MIND[1]

*   *   *

WHAT IS THINKING?

THOUGHT IS THE RESPONSE OF
MEMORY — EXPERIENCE — KNOWLEDGE
WHICH ARE ALWAYS OLD
THOUGHT IS NEVER NEW[1]

*   *   *

BEWARE OF THOUGHT

INTELLECTUALS ADORE THOUGHT

*

LOOKING VERY CLOSELY
AT THE PROCESS OF THOUGHT
HOWEVER REASONABLE AND LOGICAL IT IS
IT IS STILL THE RESPONSE OF MEMORY

*   *

THEREFORE THOUGHT IS ALWAYS OLD
AND CAN NEVER BRING FREEDOM[2]

*   *   *

THE RESTLESS MIND

THE MIND IS LIKE A MACHINE

THAT IS WORKING DAY AND NIGHT

CHATTERING EVERLASTINGLY

BUSY WHETHER ASLEEP OR AWAKE

SPEEDY AND RESTLESS

AS THE SEA[1]

*   *   *

SELF KNOWLEDGE

THE ACTION AND REACTION

OF THE MIND, OF THOUGHT

ARE ALMOST SIMULTANEOUS AND AUTOMATIC

*

SELF KNOWLEDGE COMES

WITH THE SLOWING DOWN

OF THE MIND[2]

*   *   *

THOUGHT

THINKING IS AN INDISPENSABLE FACULTY
IN THE MOVEMENT OF LIVING

*

HOWEVER THE POWER OF THOUGHT
IS NOT THE ULTIMATE WAY TO
PERFECTION[1]

*   *   *

FREEDOM IS NOT ATTAINED
BY A MIND CAUGHT IN THOUGHT
THOUGHT BEING A RESPONSE TO
MEMORY, KNOWLEDGE AND EXPERIENCE
AND THEREFORE A PRODUCT OF THE PAST

*   *

FREEDOM CAN ONLY BE ATTAINED
IN THE ACTIVE LIVING PRESENT[2]

*   *   *

SEEKING VERSUS SEARCHING

SEEKING IS CONFINED TO THE

ACTIVE MIND

TO FIND SOMETHING ALREADY KNOWN

SOMETHING WITHIN THE BORDERS OF THE MIND[1]

*   *

SEARCHING IS A STATE OF THE

QUIET MIND

AN AWAKENED, FREE AND OPEN MIND

NOT BURDENED BY THE.NETWORK OF THOUGHT

*

IT IS LIKE PLOWING A FIELD

ONE LAYS THE FURROWS AND PREPARES THE FIELD

BUT SUBSEQUENT GROWTH COMES BY ITSELF

AT THE PROPER TIME[2]

*   *   *

MAN'S CONSCIOUSNESS

CONSCIOUSNESS IS COMMON TO ALL MANKIND
HUMAN CONSCIOUSNESS IS ONE WHOLE
YOUR CONSCIOUSNESS IS THE CONSCIOUSNESS
OF ALL HUMANITY

*

DON'T TAKE THIS AS A VERBAL STATEMENT
OR YOU WILL NOT SEE ITS DEEP SIGNIFICANCE

*   *

REALIZING THAT YOU *ARE* THE REST OF MANKIND
YOU WILL HAVE BROKEN THROUGH THE NARROW CIRCLE
OF THE "ME" AND THE "YOU" — THE "I" AND "THEY"[1]

*   *   *

THE UNCONSCIOUS MIND

THE CONSCIOUS MIND MUST BE STILL

IN ORDER TO RECEIVE THE PROJECTION

OF THE UNCONSCIOUS

*

WHEN THERE IS THIS UNDERSTANDING

THE CONSCIOUS MIND

BECOMES SPONTANEOUSLY QUIET

*

FOLLOWING EVERY THOUGHT AND FEELING

BRINGS ABOUT TRANQUILITY

*   *

A MAN WHO IS FULLY AWARE IS MEDITATING[1]

*   *   *

TRANQUILITY

WHEN THE SUPERFICIAL CONSCIOUS MIND
IS FULLY AWARE OF ITS ACTIVITIES
FOLLOWING EVERY THOUGHT AND FEELING
AN UNDERSTANDING ARISES
WHICH LEADS TO SPONTANEOUS PEACE AND QUIET
AND THEN
THE UNMEASURABLE COMES INTO BEING[1]

* * *

SILENCE

IS A TRUE UNDERSTANDING OF
BEAUTY — LOVE — VIRTUE — DEATH[2]

* * *

<u>NEGATIVE THINKING</u>

IS THE HIGHEST FORM OF INTELLIGENCE

ONLY THROUGH NEGATION

DOES ONE FIND WHAT IS POSITIVE[1]

*

THE MIND BEING LIMITED TO OPERATING

WITHIN THE REALM OF

ACCUMULATED KNOWLEDGE AND EXPERIENCE

NEGATIVE THINKING WILL AVOID

PROCEEDING ALONG IDEAS

ALREADY STORED BY THE MIND

WHICH WILL NOT ALLOW DEVELOPMENT

OF NEW INTELLIGENCE[2]

*   *   *

FROM DISORDER TO ORDER

STRIVING FOR ORDER

BY A DISORDERLY MIND

CANNOT BRING ABOUT ORDER

*

BUT INSTEAD

OBSERVING DISORDER

LEADS TO INTELLIGENCE OF THAT

WHICH IS TRUE[1]

* *

MORALITY IS ONLY

THE BEGINNING OF ORDER[2]

*

THE SELF

BEING PUT TOGETHER

BY THOUGHT

IS THE ROOT CAUSE OF DISORDER[3]

* * *

ERUDITION

IS NOT THE APOGEE OF INTELLECT

NOR TO BE CLEVER, SMART OR COMPLEX

*   *

TO SEE OURSELVES AS WE ARE

REQUIRES GREAT SIMPLICITY OF MIND[1]

*   *   *

KNOWLEDGE

THERE IS NO PERFECT KNOWLEDGE

SINCE KNOWLEDGE IS ALWAYS INCOMPLETE

*   *

SINCE THOUGHT'S ACTIVITY

DEPENDS ON KNOWLEDGE

THOUGHT IS NOT INTELLIGENCE[2]

*   *   *

INTELLIGENCE

THE CEASELESS ACTIVITY OF THOUGHT

DOES NOT LEAD TO INTELLIGENCE

INTELLIGENCE LIES BEYOND THOUGHT

* *

INSTEAD IT IS

TREMENDOUSLY ALIVE TRANQUILITY

BY A FREE AND UNOCCUPIED MIND

LEADING TO PERCEPTION

OF THAT WHICH IS TRUE[1]

* * *

CREATIVITY

IT IS ONLY IN FREEDOM
THAT CREATION COMES INTO BEING

*

THEREFORE DESTRUCTION IS ESSENTIAL
NOT OF BUILDINGS OR THINGS
BUT OF ALL PSYCHOLOGICAL
DEFENCES — DEVICES — GODS — BELIEFS
AND DEPENDENCE ON
PRIESTS — EXPERIENCES — KNOWLEDGE

*

THE UNKNOWABLE ESSENCE OF THE WHOLE
IS NEVER THE EXPRESSION OF THE PART

*

IT CEASES TO BE WHEN INDIVIDUALITY
WITH ITS CAPACITY AND TECHNIQUE
BECOMES DOMINANT[1]

*   *   *

SCIENCE

SCIENCE IS THE MOVEMENT OF KNOWLEDGE

IT CALLS FOR ALWAYS MORE

*

HOWEVER KNOWLEDGE BEING LIMITED

INSIGHT AND CREATIVITY

CAN ONLY FLOURISH

IN THE ABSENCE OF THOUGHT[1]

*   *   *

INVENTION VERSUS CREATION

INVENTION

IS TOTALLY DIFFERENT FROM

CREATION

*

INVENTION IS ESSENTIALLY BASED ON

KNOWLEDGE

KNOWLEDGE BEING EVER LIMITED

INVENTION IS INEVITABLY LIMITED

*

CREATION IS NOT[1]

*   *   *

<u>DRUGS</u>

A MIND, INFLUENCED BY DRUGS

THOUGH IT MAY TEMPORARILY BECOME VERY SHARP

AND SEE SOMETHING VERY CLEARLY

WHAT IT SEES IS ITS OWN CONDITIONING

ITS OWN PETTINESS ENLARGED[1]

*   *   *

CATEGORY NO. 4

SILENCE & SPACE

THE QUIET MIND

MEDITATION

*

= Pages 48 to 59 =

* * *

SILENCE

SILENCE ACQUIRED IN FREEDOM
HAS QUITE A DIFFERENT QUALITY
THAN SILENCE BROUGHT ABOUT BY THOUGHT

*

THIS YOU WILL HAVE TO FIND OUT
FOR YOURSELF

* *

IF YOU ARE INWARDLY QUIET
IN YOUR HEART
THEN YOU HAVE LOVE AND BEAUTY
BEYOND EXPRESSION[1]

* * *

THE SILENT SPACE

WHERE THERE IS SILENCE THERE IS SPACE
SILENCE HAS THE EXTRAORDINARY ENERGY
OF THE UNIVERSE

* *

THE BUSINESS MAN IS OCCUPIED WITH COMMERCE
THE POLITICIAN WITH HIS PARTY POLITICS
THE PRIEST WITH HIS OWN NONSENSE
ALL ARE OCCUPIED AND HAVE NO SPACE[1]

* * *

THE SUPREME IMMENSITY

SILENCE IS NEITHER

THE PRODUCT OF NOISE

NOR THE CESSATION OF NOISE

INSTEAD, SILENCE COMES NATURALLY

WHEN ONE HAS ARRIVED AT

A TRUE UNDERSTANDING OF

BEAUTY, LOVE, VIRTUE AND DEATH

*

WHEN THERE IS SUCH A SILENCE

THERE BECOMES A SPACE

WHICH IS NO LONGER MEASURABLE BY THOUGHT

AN IMMENSITY WHICH IS SUPREME

AND WHICH CANNOT BE INVITED[1]

*   *   *

MEDITATION

THE MEDITATIVE STATE IS ONE OF
COMPLETE SILENCE OF THE MIND

*

TO REACH THE MEDITATIVE STATE
ONE MUST BE ABLE TO STOP THOUGHT
BUT WITHOUT THOUGHT DOING THE STOPPING

*

WITH ONE THOUGHT TRYING TO STOP ANOTHER
THIS REPRESENTS A CONFLICT
AND UNDER THOSE CONDITIONS
THE MEDITATIVE STATE CANNOT EXIST[1]

*   *   *

MEDITATION

MEDITATION IS NOT
A MEANS TO PRODUCE A RESULT
IT IS A DIMENSION
THAT IS NOT THE PROJECTION OF
ONE'S OWN LITTLE MIND

* *

IF MEDITATION IS WITH INTENT
THE DESIRED RESULT MAY BE ACHIEVED
BUT THEN IT IS NOT MEDITATION
IT IS ONLY THE FULFILLMENT OF DESIRE[1]

* *

MEDITATION USED WITH INTENT
BY SCHOOLS OF MEDITATION
IS AN ESCAPE FROM LIFE[2]

* *

"ORDINARY" MEDITATION
IS NO MORE THAN SELF HYPNOSIS[3]

* * *

MEDITATION

IN WHICH ANY FORM OF EFFORT IS INVOLVED
CEASES TO BE MEDITATION

*

IT IS NOT AN ACHIEVEMENT
A THING PRACTICED TO GAIN A DESIRED END
IT IS AN END IN ITSELF
THE MEDITATOR MUST COME TO AN END
FOR MEDITATION TO BE

*

MEDITATION IS NOT AN EXPERIENCE
A MEMORY GATHERED FOR FUTURE PLEASURE

*

MEDITATION IS ALWAYS THE PRESENT
WHILE THOUGHT ALWAYS BELONGS TO THE PAST

*

CONSCIOUS MEDITATION DEFINES BOUNDARIES
AND DESTROYS FREEDOM
IN FREEDOM ALONE IS THERE MEDITATION[1]

* * *

THE QUIET MIND

WITHOUT THAT QUICKLY SHIFTING MIND
WE COULD NOT LIVE
WE WOULD BECOME HERMITS
AND EVEN THEY HAVE TO EAT

*   *

DURING THE DAY, WHEN NO OTHER DEMANDS
ARE MADE ON THE MIND
DEVELOP THE QUIET MIND
IT DOES NOT HAVE TO BE A FORMAL SITTING
FOR MEDITATION TO BE

*   *

A MAN WHO IS FULLY AWARE
IS MEDITATING[1]

*   *   *

MEDITATION

MEDITATION IS NOT CONCENTRATION
TO CONCENTRATE COMPLETELY ON ONE THING
MAKES THE MIND LOSE
ITS ELASTICITY, ITS SHARPNESS
BECOMING INCAPABLE OF GRASPING
THE TOTAL FIELD OF LIFE[2]

*   *   *

MEDITATION

THE BEGINNING OF MEDITATION IS TO REALIZE

THAT ONE DOES NOT WANT TO ATTAIN ANYTHING

ONE MUST SIMPLY AND DISPASSIONATELY

EXAMINE THE SITUATION

AND FOLLOW THE ANTICS OF THE MIND

*

IT IS LIKE PLOWING A FIELD

ONE LAYS THE FURROWS AND PREPARES THE FIELD

BUT SUBSEQUENT GROWTH COMES BY ITSELF

AT THE PROPER TIME

*

IT IS ALL IMPORTANT TO CLEAR THE MIND

OF ALL AMBITION

AND ASK ONESELF

FOR WHAT DO I WANT THIS OR THAT RESULT?

*   *

ONCE STARTED ON MEDITATION

ON THE RIGHT FOOTING

EVERYTHING FOLLOWS BY ITSELF

WITHOUT A PRESCRIBED PROCEDURE[1]

*   *   *

MEDITATION

IF THERE IS NO MEDITATION
YOU ARE FOREVER A SLAVE OF TIME
WHO'S SHADOW IS SORROW[1]

*

LIFE IS NOT WORTH LIVING
WITHOUT MEDITATION[2]

*

MEDITATION IS PERHAPS
THE GREATEST ART IN LIFE[3]

*   *   *

MEDITATION

WITHOUT A SET FORMULA, CAUSE OR REASON

IS AN INCREDIBLE PHENOMENA

A GREAT EXPLOSION WHICH PURIFIES

*

ITS PURITY DEVASTATES

LEAVING NO HIDDEN CORNER

WHERE THOUGHT CAN LURK

*

ITS PURITY IS VULNERABLE

AND HAS NO RESISTANCE

LIKE LOVE

*

ITS SILENCE IS EMPTINESS

IN WHICH AND FROM WHICH

ALL THINGS FLOW[1]

*   *   *

MEDITATION

IS A STATE OF FULL AWARENESS

THROUGH FULL TRANQUILITY

*

LIKE A POOL OF WATER

IN THE EVENING

WHEN THE WIND SUBSIDES[1]

*   *   *

MEDITATION

I AM SORRY TO TALK ABOUT MYSELF

AND THE FOLLOWING SOUNDS EXTRAVAGANT

* *

ONE NIGHT I WOKE UP MEDITATING

THE SOURCE OF ALL ENERGY HAD BEEN REACHED

WITH AN EXTRAORDINARY EFFECT

PHYSICALLY AND ON THE BRAIN

THERE WAS NO DIVISION AT ALL

OF THE WORLD AND "ME"

BUT A COMPLETE SENSE OF PEACE

* *

THIS I WOULD LIKE OTHERS TO EXPERIENCE[1]

* * *

CATEGORY NO. 5

THE MEANING OF DEATH

BEING CONTINUOUS?

REINCARNATION

BEING IN TOTAL FREEDOM

*

= Pages 60 to 68 =

* * *

5

DEATH

THE CAUSE OF DEATH IS BIRTH

TO DIE IS

TO BECOME UN-BORN

THE COUNTERPART OF WHAT WE CALL LIFE

*

DEATH IS THE WITHDRAWING

OF LIFE

AS WE KNOW IT[1]

* * *

DEATH

THE BODY'S PHYSICAL DEGENERATION

LEADS TO DEATH

THEREBY ENDING THE FUNCTIONS OF BRAIN AND MIND

INCLUDING MEMORIES, KNOWLEDGE AND EXPERIENCE

*

THE BODY'S DEATH

REPRESENTS THE GREAT ACT OF PURGATION

*   *

THE "ME" BEING A CREATION OF THOUGHT

IS FEARFUL OF THE UNKNOWN OF DEATH

AND IT DOES NOT WANT TO END AT DEATH

AND IMAGINES CONTINUED LIFE

BY REINCARNATION

*

INSTEAD OF SPECULATING ABOUT AFTER LIFE

WHY NOT EXPLOIT THE MARVELOUS POSSIBILITIES

OFFERED IN THIS LIFE[1]

*   *   *

DEATH

WE IDENTIFY "LIFE" AS

THE PROCESS OF CONTINUITY

IN IDENTIFICATION AND MEMORY

CONSCIOUS AND UNCONSCIOUS

WITH ITS STRUGGLES, INCIDENTS AND EXPERIENCES

*

IN OPPOSITION TO LIFE THERE IS DEATH

WHICH PUTS AN END TO ALL THAT

*

BEING AFRAID OF DEATH

WE LOOK FOR A RELATIONSHIP BETWEEN THE TWO

THE KNOWN AND THE UNKNOWN

AND BUILD A BRIDGE LIKE REINCARNATION[1]

*   *   *

REINCARNATION

WE KNOW OF BEING BORN INTO LIFE
HOWEVER DURING OUR LIFETIME
TO KNOW WHETHER THERE IS SUCH A THING
AS REINCARNATION
CAN BE NO MORE THAN A BELIEF

*

BEING IN ANY WAY GUIDED BY A BELIEF
WOULD DETRACT FROM LIVING AND ACTING
IN ACCORDANCE WITH "WHAT-IS"[1]

*   *   *

THE BELIEF IN REINCARNATION
IS COMFORTING
IF YOU DON'T BEHAVE IN THIS LIFE
YOU HAVE ANOTHER CHANCE

*   *

RATHER THAN BELIEVING
IN REINCARNATION
BELIEVE IN THE POSSIBILITIES OF
YOUR PRESENT LIFE[2]

*   *   *

FROM LIFE TO DEATH

IS DEATH SOMETHING APART FROM LIFE?

IS LIFE YOUR IDENTIFICATION WITH

THE EXPERIENCES OF

YOUR HOME, YOUR WIFE, YOUR BANK ACCOUNT

YOUR STRUGGLES, QUARRELS AND INCIDENTS?

DO YOU EXPERIENCE YOURSELF AS

BEING CONTINUOUS?

*

THEN DEATH IS THE END AND OPPOSITE OF LIFE

WHICH FRIGHTENS YOU

*

YOU THEREFORE BUILD A BRIDGE, A BELIEF

THE BELIEF BEING REINCARNATION

* *

THE ENTITY, SEEKING THROUGH REINCARNATION

TO BE CONTINUOUS

CAN NEVER FIND THE NEW BECAUSE

ONLY IN THE ENDING CAN THE NEW BE FOUND

*

THE CONTINUOUS ENTITY SEEKING THE NEW

CAN FIND THE NEW ONLY

BY ENDING, BY DEATH[1]

* * *

REINCARNATION

THE SO-CALLED INTUITION

CONCERNING THE TRUTH OF REINCARNATION

OR LIFE AFTER DEATH

MAY BE MERELY A WISH FOR SURVIVAL

THESE REASONINGS, INTUITIONS AND EXPLANATIONS

ARE WITHIN THE FIELD OF THE MIND

*

THESE DESIRES TO SURVIVE

THROUGH THE NATION, FAMILY, NAME OR BELIEFS

ARE STILL THE CRAVING

FOR ONE'S OWN CONTINUITY

* *

THESE COMPLEX RESISTANCES AND HOPES

MUST VOLUNTARILY, EFFORTLESSLY AND HAPPILY

COME TO AN END[1]

* * *

DYING OF THE KNOWN

DYING PSYCHOLOGICALLY EACH DAY
TO ALL ONE'S MEMORIES, EXPERIENCES
KNOWLEDGE AND HOPES

*

NOT TO GATHER BUT TO DIE EACH DAY
IS TIMELESS BEING

*

THAT WHICH CONTINUES CAN NEVER KNOW
THE BLISS OF THE UNKNOWN[1]

*   *   *

DYING PSYCHOLOGICALLY
EVERY DAY
TO EVERY THING ONE HAS KNOWN
MAKES THE MIND
FRESH, YOUNG, AND INNOCENT[2]

*   *   *

TO "DIE" WHILE LIVING

DEATH IS AS IMPORTANT AS LIVING

IT FREES ONE TOTALLY

FROM ALL ATTACHMENTS

TO GODS, TO FUTURE, TO PAST

FROM ALL AND ANYTHING

MAN HAS PUT TOGETHER

*   *

THEN LIVING IS DYING AND

EACH NEW DAY YOU ARE INCARNATING

EACH DAY IS A NEW DAY

*

BEING IN TOTAL FREEDOM

PRODUCES ENORMOUS STRENGTH

VITALITY AND LOVE[1]

*   *   *

LOVE AND DEATH

TO UNDERSTAND LOVE AND DEATH
IS OF GREAT IMPORTANCE

*

THERE IS NO UNDERSTANDING OF LOVE
WITHOUT UNDERSTANDING OF WHAT DEATH IS

*

TO UNDERSTAND WHAT DEATH IS
ONE MUST FIRST UNDERSTAND
WHAT LIVING IS
WHICH NEEDS GREAT CLARITY OF PERCEPTION

*   *

TO UNDERSTAND WHAT LIVING IS
WE MUST BANISH THE IDEA
OF WHAT LIVING SHOULD BE

*

INSTEAD WE NEED THE SENSITIVITY
AND COMPASSION AND AFFECTION
WHICH THE INTELLECT DENIES[1]

*   *   *

CATEGORY NO. 6

BEING TRULY RELIGIOUS

ORGANIZED & COMFORTING BELIEF

IDEALIZED SUFFERING

BEING SPOON-FED

GOD THE UNKNOWN

*

* * *

6

RELIGION

PROBABLY FROM TIME IMMEMORIAL

MAN HAS BEEN ASKING HIMSELF

WHETHER THERE IS SOMETHING

SACRED, NOT WORLDLY, A REALITY, A TIMELESS STATE

SOMETHING DIVINE, HOLY, IMPERISHABLE

* *

ORGANIZED RELIGION

SEEMED TO HAVE SUPPLIED THE ANSWER

TO WHAT IT CONSIDERS TO BE THE REAL

*

AND MAN IS LED ASTRAY[1]

* * *

THE STORY ABOUT THE DEVIL

The devil was walking down the street with a friend; they saw a man ahead stoop down and pick up something from the road. As he picked it up and looked at it there was a great delight in his face. The friend of the devil asked what it was that he had picked up and the devil said, "it is truth". The friend said, "isn't that very bad business for you?" The devil answered, "Not at all, I am going to help him organize it."[1]

————————

RELIGION

RELIGION IS NOT
ORGANIZED BELIEF
RELIGION IS A STATE OF MIND[1]

*

THE RELIGIOUS MIND
IS NOT
A MIND THAT BELIEVES IN RELIGION
IT IS A STATE OF MIND WITHOUT ANY BELIEF
THEREFORE FREE FROM FEAR
GUIDED ONLY BY WHAT ACTUALLY IS[2]

*

THE RELIGIOUS MIND
IS FREE FROM PREJUDICE
FROM TRADITION AND
FROM ALL SENSE OF DIRECTION[3]

*   *

MAN HAS ALWAYS SOUGHT
SOMETHING BEYOND THE DAILY TRAVAIL
BE IT BY FEAR OR FOR SEEKING A REWARD[4]

*   *   *

BEING COMFORTED

THE URGE TO BE COMFORTED BREEDS ILLUSIONS

IT CREATES CHURCHES, TEMPLES AND MOSQUES

WE GET LOST IN THEM

AND THE REAL THING GOES BY.[1]

* * *

THE COMFORTING RELIGION

WHAT HAS MADE MAN GIVE

ENORMOUS TREASURE TO HIS TEMPLE OR CHURCH?

WAS IT FEAR OR DESIRE FOR A REWARD?

PRAYING FOR A REFRIGERATOR OR CAR

OR A BETTER WIFE OR HUSBAND?

* *

GOD AND MONEY ARE ALWAYS TOGETHER

THE CHURCHES AND TEMPLES HAVE ENORMOUS TREASURE[2]

* *

ALL ORGANIZED BELIEFS

ARE BASED ON SEPARATION

THOUGH THEY MAY PREACH BROTHERHOOD[3]

* * *

SUFFERING AND LOVE

THE CHRISTIAN WORLD

HAS IDEALIZED SUFFERING

HAS PUT IT ON A CROSS

AND WORSHIPPED IT

IMPLYING THAT YOU CAN NEVER ESCAPE FROM IT

EXCEPT THROUGH THAT ONE PARTICULAR DOOR

*   *

THIS BEING THE STRUCTURE

OF AN EXPLOITING RELIGIOUS SOCIETY

*   *

SUFFERING AND LOVE CANNOT GO TOGETHER[1]

*   *   *

RITUALS AND CEREMONIES

ARE UNNECESSARY FOR SPIRITUAL GROWTH

LET LIFE ITSELF

BE YOUR GURU, GUIDE AND MEDIATOR[2]

*   *   *

<u>HOPE AND PRAYER</u>

THE MIND DEVELOPS HOPE
AND PRONOUNCES PRAYER

*

A FREE AND HEALTHY MIND
WILL SCORN HOPE AND PRAYER
INSTEAD WILL FACE WHAT-IS[1]

*   *

ORGANIZED RELIGION DEPENDS
FOR ITS VERY EXISTENCE
ON OUR HOPES AND FEARS[2]

*   *   *

BELIEF

THE HUMAN MIND SEARCHES

FOR AN EXPLANATION OF LIFE'S PURPOSE

AND DEVELOPS A BELIEF

*   *

BUT WHEN BELIEF BECOMES FAITH

IT IMPEDES AN OPEN-MINDED OUTLOOK

*   *   *

FAITH

FAITH AND ITS LESSER COUSIN BELIEF

ARE OBSTACLES TO UNDERSTANDING ONE'S SELF

THEY IMPEDE TAKING FULL ADVANTAGE

OF THE POSSIBILITIES INHERENT IN LIFE[1]

*   *   *

BEING SPOON-FED

FOR CENTURIES WE HAVE BEEN SPOON-FED
BY OUR TEACHERS, OUR AUTHORITIES
OUR BOOKS AND OUR SAINTS
WE ARE SECOND-HAND PEOPLE

*   *

THROUGHOUT THEOLOGICAL HISTORY
OUR RELIGIOUS TEACHERS HAVE ASSURED US
THAT IF WE PERFORM CERTAIN RITUALS
CONFORM TO CERTAIN PATTERNS
SUPPRESS OUR DESIRES AND CONTROL OUR THOUGHTS
REFRAIN FROM SEXUAL DESIRE
WE SHALL, AFTER SUFFICIENT TORTURE
OF BODY AND MIND
FIND SOMETHING BEYOND THIS LITTLE LIFE

*   *

HOWEVER LONG YOU SEEK, SUCH A BROKEN MIND
WILL FIND ONLY ACCORDING TO ITS OWN DISTORTION[1]

*   *   *

GOD

IF YOU BELIEVE IN GOD

YOU ARE PREJUDICED

IF YOU DON'T BELIEVE IN GOD

YOU ARE PREJUDICED[1]

*

YOU CANNOT POSSIBLY KNOW GOD

BECAUSE ANYTHING YOU COULD KNOW

WOULD NOT BE GOD

*   *

GOD IS THE ENTIRE UNIVERSE

AS WELL AS ANYTHING BEYOND IT

*   *

ONLY GOD CAN KNOW GOD[2]

*   *   *

THE LOVE OF GOD

WHEN YOU SAY YOU LOVE GOD

YOU ACTUALLY LOVE

A PROJECTION OF YOUR OWN IMAGINATION

WHICH IS A PROJECTION OF YOURSELF

CLOTHED IN CERTAIN FORMS OF RESPECTABILITY

ACCORDING TO WHAT YOU THINK IS NOBLE AND HOLY

*

THEREFORE WHEN YOU WORSHIP GOD

YOU ARE WORSHIPPING YOURSELF

*

TO SAY "I LOVE GOD" IS ABSOLUTE NONSENSE[1]

* * *

MAN'S ULTIMATE PLEASURE

IS TO FIND IF THERE IS

A PERMANENT STATE IN HEAVEN

GOD BEING TO HIM

THE HIGHEST FORM OF PLEASURE[2]

* * *

CATEGORY NO. 7

THE "ME" IN ONE'S CIRCLE

OBSERVING IN FREEDOM

AWARENESS

FEAR & PLEASURE — HAPPINESS — SORROW

PEACE & SECURITY

TRADITION & MORALITY

SEX — CHASTITY — MARRIAGE

"WHAT-IS"

*

*   *   *

7

<u>FREE THE MIND</u>

WE LIVE WITHIN A CIRCLE AROUND THE "ME"
WOVEN AROUND THE KNOWLEDGE OF ONESELF

*

WE ARE AFRAID TO LOOK BEYOND OR TO LEAVE
OUR LITTLE CIRCLE
THIS BEING THE BEGINNING OF
THE PROCESS OF FEAR

*   *

ONLY BY STEPPING OUT OF THIS CIRCLE
DOES ONE LIVE IN PEACE

*   *

FREE THE MIND OF THE DIVISION
OF THE "ME" AND THE "NOT-ME"[1]

*   *   *

<u>YOU</u>

DO NOT IDENTIFY YOURSELF

WITH THE CONTENTS

AND THE I.Q.

OF THE BRAIN[1]

* *

OBSERVE YOURSELF

FROM THE "OUTSIDE"

WHICH LEADS TO FINDING YOUR PLACE

IN YOUR ENVIRONMENT[2]

* * *

THE OBSERVER AND THE OBSERVED

DO WE PUT A SCREEN

BETWEEN THE OBSERVER AND THE OBSERVED

CONSISTING OF

PREJUDICES, JUDGEMENTS AND COMPARISONS

THEREBY IMPEDING OBSERVATION?

*

WHEN THESE FALSE OBSERVATIONS SUBSIDE

BY LOOKING INTENSELY AT AN OBJECT

THE OBSERVER OBSERVES THE OBSERVED

IN FREEDOM[1]

*   *   *

CHOICELESS AWARENESS

WE MAKE AN IMAGE OF PEOPLE

OUR FRIENDS, OUR HUSBAND OR WIFE, OUR NEIGHBOR

THEY IN TURN MAKE AN IMAGE OF US

*

IMAGES ARE SUBJECTIVE CONSTRUCTIONS

FROM INCIDENTS PLEASANT OR UNPLEASANT

BY INSULT OR FLATTERY

THEY DO NOT REPRESENT A TRUE PICTURE

*

SUCH FALLACIES CAN BE AVOIDED

BY CULTIVATING AN ATTITUDE

OF CHOICELESS AWARENESS

A STATE OF PERCEPTION

FREE FROM EXPERIENCE[1]

*   *   *

FEAR

DESIRE FOR SELF PROTECTION

CREATES FEAR

*

IDENTIFICATION WITH

A COUNTRY, A RELIGION OR IDEA

IS AN ESCAPE FROM FEAR[1]

*   *   *

A MAN WHO HAS

NO SENSE OF FEAR

IS NOT AGGRESSIVE

*

HE IS A TOTALLY FREE

AND PEACEFUL

MAN[2]

*   *   *

FEAR

FEAR ONLY EXISTS IN RELATION TO SOMETHING

ONLY OF SOMETHING KNOWN

LIKE A PHYSICAL OR PSYCHOLOGICAL PAIN

*

THERE IS NO FEAR OF DEATH ITSELF

ONLY THE FEAR OF LOSING THE KNOWN BY DEATH[1]

*   *   *

ESCAPE FROM FEAR

FEAR THRIVES IN THE PROCESS OF

ACCUMULATION AND BELIEF

*

FEAR RESULTS FROM NON-ACCEPTANCE

OF WHAT-IS[2]

*   *   *

FEAR AND PLEASURE

THOUGHT PRODUCES, SUSTAINS AND NOURISHES
BOTH FEAR AND PLEASURE
WHEN THERE IS A DEMAND FOR PLEASURE
THERE MUST ALSO BE FEAR[1]

* * *

THOUGHT AND FEAR

THOUGHT IS THE ORIGIN OF FEAR
THOUGHT IS THE SOURCE OF SORROW[2]

*

PLEASURE, FEAR AND PAIN
ARE THE RESULT OF THOUGHT

*

WHEN THERE IS THE STATE OF PLEASURE OR FEAR
LOVE CEASES TO BE[3]

* * *

HAPPINESS

HAPPINESS IS NOT AN END IN ITSELF
IT COMES WITH UNDERSTANDING OF WHAT-IS

*

HAPPINESS THAT IS BOUGHT
OR ACQUIRED BY POWER OR ACTION
IS MERELY GRATIFICATION

*

HAPPINESS IS NOT REMEMBRANCE

*

HAPPINESS IS THAT STATE
WHICH COMES INTO BEING
WITH TRUTH
EVER NEW, NEVER CONTINUOUS[1]

*   *   *

SORROW

MEMORY AND TIME
ARE THE ROOT OF SORROW

*

SORROW IS SELF-CREATED[1]

*

SORROW IF CLOSELY OBSERVED
IS GENERALLY SELF-PITY[2]

*

THE ENDING OF SORROW
IS THE BEGINNING OF WISDOM[3]

*

THE ENDING OF SORROW
IS THE BEGINNING OF LOVE[4]

*   *   *

<u>PEACE</u>

PEACE IS A STATE OF MIND

IT IS THE ABSENCE OF ALL DESIRE

TO BE SECURE[1]

*   *   *

<u>SECURITY</u>

A MIND THAT IS

SAFE AND SECURE

IS A BOURGEOIS, A SHODDY MIND[2]

*   *   *

TRADITION

MOST OF US LIVE WITHIN A FRAMEWORK
OF IDEAS OF
WHAT IS RIGHT OR WHAT IS WRONG
TOLD TO US BY OUR PARENTS, IN SCHOOL,
OR BY OUR PRIEST

*   *

INSTEAD OF LIVING
WITHIN SUCH A FRAMEWORK
DISCOVER ON YOUR OWN
WHAT IS REAL AND WHAT IS TRUE
HOWEVER NOBLE OR EXCITING
YOUR TEACHER MAY BE[1]

*   *   *

PARENTS

PARENTS WANT THEIR CHILDREN TO HAVE

A SECURE POSITION IN SOCIETY

* *

WHAT THEY CALL RESPONSIBILITY

IS PART OF THAT RESPECTABILITY

WHICH THEY WORSHIP

* *

BUT RESPECTABILITY

DOES NOT LEAD TO ORDER

* *

THEY ARE CONCERNED ONLY

WITH BECOMING A PERFECT BOURGEOIS[1]

* * *

NATIONALISM

WITH ALL ITS

PATRIOTISM — ISOLATION — NARROWNESS

IS A DESTRUCTIVE POISON

IN A NATION[1]

* *

THE GOVERNMENT SAYS

GO AND KILL

FOR THE LOVE OF YOUR COUNTRY[2]

* *

THE SELF MAY IDENTIFY WITH THE NATION

BUT THAT IDENTIFICATION WITH THE GREATER

IS STILL A GLORIFICATION OF THE SELF[3]

* *

THE NATIONALIST WHO TALKS OF BROTHERHOOD

IS TELLING A LIE

HE IS IN A STATE OF CONTRADICTION[4]

* * *

<u>BEING MORAL</u>

THE MORALITY OF SOCIETY
IS NOT MORAL

*

UNLESS A MIND IS HIGHLY MORAL
AND NOT EMBEDDED IN RIGHTEOUSNESS
IT IS NOT CAPABLE OF BEING FREE[1]

*　*　*

<u>PROSPERITY</u>

PROSPERITY WITHOUT AUSTERITY
LEADS TO UNETHICAL LUXURY
AND TO A SOCIETY
WHICH IS CORRUPT AND IMMORAL[2]

*　*　*

SEX AND GOD

THE HOLY MEN MAINTAIN
THAT YOU CANNOT COME NEAR TO GOD
IF YOU INDULGE IN SEX
SO THEY PUSH IT ASIDE
ALTHOUGH THEY ARE EATEN UP WITH IT

*

THEY HAVE STARVED THEIR HEARTS AND MINDS
THEY ARE DEHYDRATED BEINGS

*   *

SUCH AUSTERITY IS A GREATER WASTE OF ENERGY
THAN INDULGING IN SEX

*

BY DENYING SEXUALITY
THEY DENY THE WHOLE BEAUTY OF THE EARTH
BECAUSE BEAUTY IS ASSOCIATED WITH WOMEN
IT DOES BRUTAL VIOLENCE
TO ALL FINER INSTINCTS[1]

*   *   *

CHASTITY

CHASTITY IS NOT A THING OF THE MIND

IT IS THE VERY NATURE OF LOVE

WITHOUT LOVE

DO WHAT YOU WILL

THERE CAN BE NO CHASTITY[1]

*   *   *

ABANDONMENT IN SEX

WHAT SEX GIVES YOU MOMENTARILY

IS TOTAL ABANDONMENT OF THE SELF[2]

*   *   *

MARRIAGE AND SEX

WHEN COUPLES MARRY TO AVOID
THEIR LONELINESS AND THEIR EMPTINESS

*

SUCH RELATIONSHIPS ARE AN ESCAPE
THEY ARE NOT BASED ON TRUE LOVE

*   *   *

IT IS HIDING A PROBLEM AND
STRENGTHENING THE LONELINESS[1]

*   *   *

<u>WHAT-IS</u>

THE IDEOLOGICAL STATE

OF NON-VIOLENCE, FREEDOM AND LOVE

DOES NOT EXIST, THAT IS JUST AN IDEA

WHAT EXISTS IS WHAT-IS

*

CAN WHAT-IS BE TRANSFORMED

WITHOUT BECOMING WHAT-SHOULD-BE?

SUCH PURSUIT OF THE IDEAL

IS A DIVISION, A CONFLICT[1]

*   *   *

LOVE AND WHAT-IS

TO BE

HIGHLY SENSITIVE AND INTELLIGENT

AND CAPABLE OF

LOGICAL, SEQUENTIAL PERCEPTION

TO SEE

EVERYTHING CLEARLY, OBJECTIVELY

NON-EMOTIONALLY AND NON-SENTIMENTALLY

*

WILL ALLOW ONE TO DISCOVER

WHAT-IS

BEYOND THE MEASURE OF THOUGHT

CAPABLE OF THE HIGHEST FORM OF LOVE[1]

*   *   *

<u>OBSERVING "WHAT-IS"</u>

TO OBSERVE ACTUALLY WHAT-IS
THE MIND MUST BE
FREE, CLEAR AND UNDIVIDED

*

THAT IS, WITHOUT THE DIVISION OF
THE "ME" AND THE "NOT-ME"
THE "WE" AND THE "THEY"[1]

* * *

<u>THE "WHAT-IS"</u>

TRUTH IS NOT "WHAT-IS"
THE UNDERSTANDING OF "WHAT-IS"
OPENS THE DOOR TO TRUTH[2]

* * *

CATEGORY NO. 8

THE ETERNAL TRUTH

THE STATE OF SEARCH

THE NAMELESS REALITY

THE TIMELESS STATE OF CREATIVITY

TIME

INFINITY — ETERNITY — ORIGINLESS

*

= Pages 99 to 108 =

*   *   *

<u>TRUTH</u>

TRUTH IS NOT

SOMETHING PERMANENT, SOMETHING FIXED

THEREFORE IT CANNOT BE SOUGHT

TRUTH IS A LIVING THING

IT IS THE STATE OF SEARCH[1]

* *

TRUTH IS SOMETHING

THAT IS ALWAYS NEW

THEREFORE THE MIND CANNOT COME TO IT

WITH A CONCLUSION, AN OPINION OR A JUDGEMENT

THE MIND MUST BE FREE

FOR TRUTH TO BE[2]

* * *

TRUTH

ONLY A MIND THAT IS
INNOCENT AND VULNERABLE
CAN SEE WHAT TRUTH IS[1]

*

TRUTH IS LIMITLESS
IT CANNOT BE ORGANIZED
BY ANY SECT OR RELIGION
IT CANNOT BE NARROWED DOWN
AND MADE A PLAYTHING FOR THE WEAK

*

RATHER THAN TRUTH BEING BROUGHT DOWN
THE INDIVIDUAL MUST MAKE AN EFFORT
TO ASCEND TO IT[2]

*   *

TRUTH IS A PATHLESS LAND
IT CANNOT BE REACHED BY ANY PATH

*

IF ORGANIZED
IT BECOMES CRYSTALLIZED, DEAD[3]

*   *   *

THE ETERNAL TRUTH

SHOULD THE "I" BE ABLE TO REACH
THE ETERNAL TRUTH
SUCH BECOMING CONTAINS THE ELEMENTS OF TIME
WHILE TRUTH OF NECESSITY
CONTAINS NO ELEMENT OF TIME

*

THIS CONTRADICTION REVEALS A FALLACY
THE PROCESS OF THE "I" BECOMING
IS THEREFORE AN ILLUSION

* *

TO REACH THE TRUTH BY A PROCESS
REQUIRING THE AID OF A TEACHER
PERPETUATES THE "I"
AND IS THEREFORE MISLEADING

* *

INSTEAD THE ONLY WAY TO COME UPON TRUTH
IS BY THE SILENCE OF MEDITATION[1]

* * *

REALITY

REALITY IS A TIMELESS STATE

IN WHICH TIME IS NOT A FUNDAMENTAL PARAMETER

A STATE IN WHICH EVERYTHING "IS" SIMULTANEOUSLY

BUT NOT NECESSARILY MANIFESTING:

THE PAST, THE PRESENT, THE FUTURE AND THE NONE

A STATE WHICH THE MIND CANNOT MEASURE

*

ONE CAN NO MORE KNOW REALITY

THAN ONE CAN KNOW GOD

GOD BEING THE SUPREME REALITY[1]

*   *   *

REALITY

REALITY IS A TIMELESS STATE

TO ENCOUNTER REALITY

ONE MUST BE FREE OF ALL

BELIEF — FEAR — GREED

ENVY — BRUTALITY — CONFLICT

AMBITION — COMPETITION

ONLY THEN CAN ONE FIND OUT

WHETHER THERE IS

THE ETERNAL — THE NAMELESS[1]

* * *

<u>CREATIVITY</u>

DOES NOT COME ABOUT

BY SELF-CENTERED ACTIVITY OF THE MIND

*

IT IS AN EXTRAORDINARY STATE

IN WHICH THERE IS NO ELEMENT OF TIME

OR RECOGNITION OF

OR IDENTIFICATION WITH

THE "ME"

*   *

A TIMELESS STATE

A STATE WHICH OPENS THE DOOR TO LOVE[1]

*   *   *

THE ORIGIN OF TIME

PSYCHOLOGICAL TIME

(TIME NOT BY THE CLOCK)

ORIGINATED WHEN MAN DEVELOPED

THE SENSE OF THE "I" AND THE "ME"

WHICH ENGENDERED THE WISH TO "BECOME"

SOMETHING WHICH REPRESENTED

THE ELEMENT OF TIME[1]

* *

THOUGHT AND TIME

TIME IS THE PRODUCT OF THOUGHT

WITHOUT THE THINKING PROCESS

TIME IS NOT

THE MIND IS THE MAKER OF TIME

* *

THE ENDING OF TIME IS MEDITATION[2]

* * *

TIME

TIME IS MEMORY
ECSTASY IS TIMELESS

*

THE BLISS OF MEDITATION
HAS NO DURATION
IT IS ONLY A SECOND BY THE WATCH
IN WHICH THERE IS
THE WHOLE MOVEMENT OF LIFE
WITHOUT A BEGINNING AND END

*   *

IN MEDITATION THE SECOND IS THE INFINITE[1]

*   *   *

INFINITY — ETERNITY — ORIGINLESS

IT IS IMPOSSIBLE TO UNDERSTAND THESE
EXTRAPOLATIONS OF THE KNOWABLE.
THEY SURPASS THE FUNCTION OF THE BRAIN
AND REQUIRE A STATE BEYOND THE CEREBRAL.[1]

* * *

WHENCE CREATION?

THE ORIGIN OF ALL LIFE IS NAMELESS

NO DESCRIPTION CAN EVER DESCRIBE

THE ORIGIN

IT IS ABSOLUTELY QUIET

*   *

CREATION IS SOMETHING MOST HOLY

THE MOST SACRED THING IN LIFE[1]

*   *   *

Note: These were the last words spoken in public (Madras)
by J. Krishnamurti in his present life, which ended
on Feb. 17, 1986 at Ojai, Cal.

BIBLIOGRAPHIC

SOURCES

BY FOOTNOTES

NOTE

Occasionally a paragraph has been inserted which is not a verse-like condensation of a pulished statement by Krishnamurti but instead either spoken by Krishnamurti to the compiler of this booklet or so inspired and the title is then marked as -S-. Occasionally the source was not available (N) at the time of this printing but the bibliography will be completed in successive printings. The notations H and P stand for HARDBACK or PAPERBACK.

B

V	1	BULLETIN 53	K. FOUNDATION OJAI, CA.	1986	P	5
VI	1	BULLETIN 53	K. FOUNDATION OJAI, CA	1986	P	14
VII	1	YOU ARE THE WORLD	HARPER & ROW	1972	P	77-78
	2	-S-				
1	1	-S-				
2	1	YOU ARE THE WORLD	HARPER & ROW	1972	P	104
3	1	LIFE AHEAD	HARPER & ROW	1963	H	124
4	1	YOU ARE THE WORLD	HARPER & ROW	1972	P	74-75
5	1	YOU ARE THE WORLD	HARPER & ROW	1972	P	9
	2	N				
6	1	COMMENTARIES ON LIVING-2	HARPER BROS.	1958	H	70-71
7	1	COMMENTARIES ON LIVING-2	HARPER BROS.	1958	H	70
8	1	YOU ARE THE WORLD	HARPER & ROW	1972	P	62
9	1	YOU ARE THE WORLD	HARPER & ROW	1972	P	59
10	1	YOU ARE THE WORLD	HARPER & ROW	1972	P	75
11	1	YOU ARE THE WORLD	HARPER & ROW	1972	P	75
12	1	THE NETWORK OF THOUGHT	MIRANANDA	1982	P	11
13	1	N				
14	1	YOU ARE THE WORLD	HARPER & ROW	1972	P	141
15	1	YOU ARE THE WORLD	HARPER & ROW	1972	P	29
	2	-S-				
16	1	COMMENTARIES ON LIVING	HARPER BROS.	1958	H	91
17	1	N				
	2	N				
18	1	YOU ARE THE WORLD	HARPER & ROW	1972	P	30
19	1	COMMENTARIES ON LIVING-3	GOLLANCZ	1961	H	60
	2	COMMENTARIES ON LIVING-2	HARPER BROS.	1958	H	70
	3	COMMENTARIES ON LIVING-2	HARPER BROS.	1058	H	18
20	1	YOU ARE THE WORLD	HARPER & ROW	1972	P	80
	2	YOU ARE THE WORLD	HARPER & ROW	1972	P	86
	3	-S-				
21	1	FREEDOM FROM THE KNOWN	HARPER & ROW	1969	H	135-136
22	1	YOU ARE THE WORLD	HARPER & ROW	1972	P	166
23	1	LIFE AHEAD	HARPER & ROW	1963	H	Jacket
	2	BULLETIN 53	K. FOUND. OJAI, CA	1986	P	13-14
	3	LIFE AHEAD	HARPER & ROW	1963	H	72
24	1	YOU ARE THE WORLD	HARPER & ROW	1972	P	94
25	1	YOU ARE THE WORLD	HARPER & ROW	1972	P	168
26	1	YOU ARE THE WORLD	HARPER & ROW	1972	P	67
	2	YOU ARE THE WORLD	HARPER & ROW	1972	P	30
	3	N				
27	1	N				
	2	THE FIRST & LAST FREEDOM	GOLLANCZ	1961	H	86
28	1	YOU ARE THE WORLD	HARPER & ROW	1972	P	30
29	1	AT THE FEET OF THE MASTER	THEOS. PUBL. CO.	1927	H	10